Love's Sonnets

Interpreting the interminable interloper.

Written by Alex Burrett
Cover design and typeset by Julian Burrett

Published by Fedw

Dedicated to Gorse, Morgan, Scarlett, Mitchell and Lauren.
And loved others.

With thanks to all those (in addition to those named above) who supported my endeavour of writing and blogging this project: Malc, Andy, Marcus, Caroline, Andrea, Will, Julian, Jim, Shane, Laurel, Charlene, Lone, Danny, Lisa, Dominique, James, Bambos, Gemma, Anita.

www.lovessonnets.com
(features readings of each sonnet)

Love's Sonnets

Love's Sonnets

Sonnets are English language's haiku. The sonnet's form (14 lines of iambic pentameter) is strictly defined. As is the Shakespearian rhyme scheme: ababcdcdefefgg.

Love, on the other hand, is indefinable – despite being the emotion that most impacts our lives; when Survival is off duty, Love wrestles with Logic for control of our tiller.

Over 14 months during 2021 & 2022, I wrote a sonnet a week and published it on a blog: lovessonnets.com. This book presents the result of that endeavour.

There are four collections of fourteen love sonnets. Each sonnet is preceded with a commentary on the writing process, language techniques and structure.

Each collection has a different theme. The first theme is **Personification**, the second **Forms of Love** (inspired by the several Ancient Greek words for love), the third **Ages and Sins** (Shakespeare's seven ages of man plus the seven deadly sins), and the final is **Love Letters** (letters to people and things I love or have loved).

These are not love sonnets. They are Love's Sonnets. They belong to Love. They are its facets, its characteristics, its foibles.

Contents

Personification collection

Forms of Love collection

Ages and Sins collection

Love Letters collection

Personification collection

Personification is the act of attributing human qualities to inhuman things. And what could be both more human and more inhuman than love?

Love is often depicted as childish, angelic or gentle. Sometimes all three. So, for my first 'personification' sonnet, I imagined love as a gigantic creature – one capable of grabbing Cupid in its fist and squeezing the arrows out of it.

To make it clear Love is not Cupid, I refer to the latter as a 'flighty flirt god'. This diminishes the status of Cupid as the personification of love and also creates onomatopoeia with the sound of Cupid's wings.

I was tempted to include a Shakespearian nob gag but, in almost the words of Robert Frost, 'kept the impulse for another day' – declining to replace 'kissed' with 'pricked'. (The result being more inclusive as well as less vulgar.)

'Mask' was not an intentional reference to the Covid pandemic: its use in this sonnet suggests an eye mask rather than one worn over the mouth. However, since creative works partly reveal the subconscious, I cannot deny the possibility of this association.

Two lines in the final couplet of my original draft ended with half rhymes. My nine-year-old son let me know this was less than satisfactory, so I changed them to perfect rhymes. I am far happier with the result.

So here's the first sonnet of my planned year-long project.

Love is a Beast

Love is a beast that crushes doting hearts;
Can catch the flighty flirt god in its fist
And force that youth to loose his lightweight darts –
A needle storm, with every dreamer kissed.
They say Love's blind, they're right, but not by choice:
It does not wear a mask through which it peeks,
But feels instead for prey, then with full voice
Roars to declare it owns the souls it seeks.
Love backs off not from armies in bold garb
Nor flees when discord mountains do erupt.
Its Titan hide cannot be pierced by barbs;
No poison can its monstrous heart corrupt.
      But tiny sparks do not fear Love's great size,
      Its thick arms fan the fire so flames can rise.

Love isn't always what it seems. Sometimes we imagine
it is reciprocated… when it isn't. Even worse, we can
be deceived. We can believe someone loves us when their
true agenda is exploitative. In this sonnet, I personify false
love as the conjurer – the character that intends to mislead.
(Loki, if you likie.)

Sonnets thrive on words that are spelt and/or sound the same
but have different meanings: homonyms and homophones.
Having such a word in a heading is like a springboard
that lets a vaulter rise higher and do more tricks.

I start with the dual meaning of 'fool' being both someone
who is stupid and someone who does the fooling.
The heading might suggest that Love is stupid; the sonnet
rapidly asserts the other meaning. But, as is always the case
with homonyms and homophones, the other sense is never
truly discarded.

After establishing Love as the Shakespearian fool (the jester
who is also knowing), I develop the character of duplicitous
Love in the poem by adding further, more insidious,
descriptions. The Love that begins as a (possibly foolish)
clown, becomes an enchanter, a hypnotist and
a spiritual parasitoid.

Love is a Fool

L ove is a fool with bells tied to its hat
That dances drunk to desperado drums:
Brash beats that bowl our senses' fences flat,
Confounding booms that shatter walls to crumbs.
Path made, the fool skips barricades laid low –
Conniving clown to need such bombardments;
Distractions that appear to please but sow
Infected seeds of future punishments.
The trickster next scoops you up in its arms;
Emblazoned sleeves of an enchanter's cloak
Adorned with glinting jewels and fancy charms
That hypnotise till you become the joke.
      Once gripped you'll wither feebly to a ghost,
      Unless you spot the fraud of your false host.

'Love stands with Death' explores the similar ways in which we respond to love and death. They both make us cry, both cause us to think deeply about others that are close to us, both feed on human need. We fear the end of one and the arrival of the other. Both have the power to make us mourn.

My poetic exploration of the similarities between these two concepts encompasses how we respond to, celebrate and rely on these two awkward bedfellows. I created images that have dual meanings such as 'Believers' paths with blossom petals strewn' and 'Pure flesh discoloured with voracious bites'. These could be descriptions of the impact of either Love or Death.

Whilst the first two quatrains play on the similarities between Love and Death, the third and final quatrain brings them into conflict with one another. They become two gladiators chained together. In mortal combat.

But the final couplet brings both twist and resolution – as the final couplet of a sonnet often does. Neither of these personifications will be allowed to perish because human existence depends on, and is hugely defined by, both Love and Death.

Love stands with Death

Love stands with Death. They prey on common fears:
The end of things, the acrid taste of loss,
Crushed shells of dreams, evaporated tears,
The barb that knows the aim but not the cost.
Love trips with Death. They witness the same sights:
Believers' paths with blossom petals strewn,
Pure flesh discoloured with voracious bites,
Crazed souls that wander blinded by the moon.
Love fights with Death when their desires collide;
Wild gladiators armed with sword and shield,
Who slash their blades while to each other tied
With chains so neither can escape. Nor yield.
      But when each battle's fought, the thumb is raised;
      The mob would sure erupt if one's erased.

'Love loves not those' is dedicated to unrequited love. Love is personified in this sonnet as a character who is indifferent to the wants and needs of those who love or depend on it.

We all have the right not to love someone back: being aware of that fact doesn't make it easier for the one who's doing the adoring.

In this sonnet, I depict unrequited Love as a colonist admiral – a sort of Walter Raleigh figure. My colonist admiral is egotistical, aloof, hungry for conquest. (I imagine most were.) Each quatrain depicts a different scene in Love's conquering mission: the departure, the journey across the ocean and arrival at another country. These stages are chronological. This is not necessary in a sonnet with narrative elements, but I find it rewarding to structure sonnets this way.

The final couplet delivers advice to the admirer who, throughout the sonnet, is represented by adoring crowds, drowning sailors and smitten foes.

Love loves not those

Love loves not those that flock to its parades:
Whose glazed eyes scan the medals on its chest,
Whose reaching arms form flimsy barricades,
Who, when they're waved away, think they are blessed.
Love's captain of a fleet – attack flag high
Who will not change the course for drowning souls.
Compassion signals flap at its blind eye;
Distress won't turn this ardent from its goals.
Love casts off nagging burdens, then it leaps
To conquer virgin lands and pastures new.
It flinches not for smitten souls it reaps
Whose flimsy fractured armour rusts with dew
      Narcissus Love needs reverence to thrive
      Refuse to fuel its fire, and you'll survive.

When writing a personification sonnet, I first think of a form of love I want to feature then I try to work out what type of person or creature matches that form of love. For this sonnet I wanted to explore hidden love, love that is intentionally buried deep within us.

A miner seemed a suitable human substitute for buried love; the first line came quickly 'Love is a miner buried underground'. As I worked through the logic of the poem, I realised a mining accident did not fit with the logic of burying a love that cannot be allowed to thrive. Unrealised love is not starved after becoming accidentally trapped somewhere.

So, rather than have a mining accident, in order to maintain the logic of the metaphor, I had this miner buried by a malevolent mine owner. Perhaps it is a raw material mine and knowledge that there are diamonds within it might threaten the essence of that facility's being. (Ourself.)

Love is a Miner

Love is a miner buried underground
Who was not trapped when a weak vein was sliced
Beneath the earth's thick skin, where ghosts abound;
But rather to this grave was sacrificed.
Love scratches at the clog with fingernails
As if the blockage was an accident.
Love shreds its knuckles when the clawing fails
Imagining light dust where there's cement.
Lost Love won't have the mercy of quick death
Nor like canary quickly suffocate.
Slowly this sap will starve and its last breath
Will fade, unseen, unheard by its sole mate.
      When Love saw hidden diamonds it was doomed.
      Now with those precious treasures it's entombed.

Although this sonnet forms one of my personification series, it is arguably zoomorphism – giving things animal, rather than human, qualities. In defence, the animal I use has the name and qualities of a famous fictional human…
Benjamin Button. I therefore feel its inclusion is vindicated.

The inspiration for this poem is that form of love that is overwhelmingly captivating at its outset, then ebbs to a faint shadow of its original self. Such love seems like a glorious butterfly at its beginning and a tiny spec of its former self at the end (an insect egg). This is the reverse lifecycle of an actual butterfly.

And what being famously lived its life in reverse? Benjamin Button. So this form of love became a Benjamin Button Butterfly. (Then, for the purpose of fitting it into iambic pentameter, Benjy Button.)

Love is a Benjy Button Butterfly

L ove is a Benjy Button Butterfly –
    A sequined tumbler flipping into view:
Whose tricks the laws of reason do defy,
Whose incandescent form sparks fires in you.
Next Benjy Button Love's a swollen beast
Engorged on all the bounty you provide;
Your palm and laurel leaves become its feast
Attempts to sate its needs are dreams defied.
Then Benjy Love's a microscopic egg
Boundless emotions bound inside a shell
A Damoclian passion powder keg
Whose fragile crust, if cracked, could unleash hell.
       But warmth instead will incubate this seed,
       And from that crumb will burst a beauty freed.

Having written a few sonnets for this collection that are, at least in part, somewhat critical of love, a more celebratory one seemed appropriate. So this sonnet celebrates nurturing love. And the person that best represents nurturing love is… the nurse. The nurturing nurse.

If we're lucky, during our lives of "seven ages", we will encounter different forms of nurture: those that bring us into the world (the midwife); our early carers (the wet nurse); the paediatric nurse who patches us up; the first aider for early bumps and scrapes; the paramedic when more substantial medical assistance is needed; the people who care for us when we are frail (the care assistant) and those who are there for our final act (the hospice nurse).

These nurses are sometimes metaphorical, sometimes literal. In this poem, a single, metamorphosising, metaphorical nurse accompanies us throughout our lives.

Love is the Nurse

Love is the nurse who guides you to the light:
Who feeds kind milk between your infant lips
Who patches wounds when realities bite
Who sets you free when you're in Fever's grips.
Love's expedition medic for your quest –
The march from womb to tomb; Love will step in
To start the heart in your deflated chest
Or dress demonic scorches in thin skin.
Then Love's your care companion when Time strikes:
The hands that keep you steady, like a crutch
The spirit boost when fear of Midnight hikes
That final, life-affirming, human touch.
       At times this nurse will other duties find
       So treasure every moment when you're twined.

'Love is a Whore' comes (if you'll excuse the pun) next in the Personification series after last week's 'Love is the Nurse'. From care to caress in just seven days! A series of poems should play like a symphony: light and shade, calm before a storm, "there should be sunshine after rain" ('Why Worry', Dire Straits).

This sonnet depicts sensual love as a whore – an embodiment of sensory and sexual stimulation. Because this whore could be either (or both) genders, it made sense that this personification of love should be genderless. And "high-class"? Well, being a bit of a snob, I found the concept of a "high-class" whore more alluring than one providing services between two wheelie bins in a car park out the back of a Wetherspoon pub.

Love is a Whore

Love's a hermaphrodite and high-class whore
Whose perfumed sent is cocaine up your nose
Whose unzipped flesh unhinges your locked jaw
Whose every sway dictates where your gaze goes.
Love's dressed undressed or dressed for your delight
In threads that dredge up long-forgotten gems
Glimpsed by a junior diver with keen sight
But ignorant of links 'tween roots and stems.
Whore Love's song's sweeter than a siren's psalm
And its plump lips electrify taste buds
Love tingles skin like seas of Tiger Balm
And a monsoon, turns arid bush to floods.
          This Love's intoxicating opium
          Its addicts are left senseless, blind and dumb.

'Born Fighter Love' is one of the more pro-love sonnets in my personification series. It began with a simple thought: Love has all the attributes of a fighter; it can inflict pain using skill, insight and experience. Logic concludes that Love is a fierce combatant. We've all experienced its ire. We've felt the pain of battling irrepressible, ferocious Love.

But, like the martial devices they use, fighters themselves are double-edged swords. One person's freedom fighter is another person's terrorist. A Parachute Regiment company commander once told me he stood as a character witness for a soldier facing charges of public affray. His defence was to explain that this solder, arrested brawling outside a pub, was doing what he had been trained to do. He had been conditioned to fight, taught to respond violently when under threat. The officer elaborated by explaining that this soldier's nation, the overarching institution of which the court system was merely a constituent part, required him to have a violent disposition.

So, in this sonnet, we have 'Born Fighter Love' – the pugilist who ignores the rules. The indefatigable, indomitable, invincible Love.

Born Fighter Love

Born Fighter Love hits like a charging ox
But do not hope for respite while it turns,
This pugilist will stand its ground and box
With flaming fists that leave bruises and burns.
Combatant Love will dumb your rattled brain,
Make your eyes stream with cochineal slush,
Land blow salvos that inflict searing pain
With force that lungs like concertinas crush.
Deft brawler Love mishears the Queensbury Rules:
Targets weak spots to knock you to your knees
Draws diamond tears to set in its Crown Jewels
It won't be turned by mournful cries, or pleas.
      No threat will make this militant retreat;
      No ally will help more when you feel beat.

'Love the Dealer' draws comparison between the effects of love and of illegal drugs. Both dilate pupils, affect our senses and change our perception of things. So, in this personification sonnet, Love is a drug dealer.

I've included several examples of the narcotic effects of both love and drugs. Both affect our vision, adding, for example, a "glow" to objects of interest. Both cause us to see forms differently – encouraging us to find beauty where others don't, or convincing us objects have proportions that are not scientifically verifiable: we might imagine immense love when it is minuscule, or vice versa.

The capping couplet of the sonnet presents two polar opposite conclusions: we should avoid the drug of love because it distorts reality; we should use it because it makes life more wonderful. The relative positioning of these two propositions suggests the latter might be the recommended option.

Love the Dealer

Love deals in drugs that in eyes black holes grow
With might to bend the beams that hold up stars,
Switch once dull forms to charms that pulse and glow,
Tear holes in time that leave fast-healing scars.
Love's drugs contort creatures to divine forms
Bring dust to life, set bacchanals on fire;
Upon the cautious tourists unleash storms,
Draw all a big band's sounds from Cupid's lyre.
That dealer in narcotics, senses twists:
Let's you taste joy and smell Desire's perfume
Compels your hands to stroke celestial mists
Makes you think you can hear bright passions bloom.
      We should decline this criminal's potions
      But who would choose small fires over suns?

The seed idea for 'Trust Quartermaster Love' was that love can assist us in many ways through life. It can give us the strength to cope with things that would otherwise overwhelm us. It can make us feel joy. It can protect us when the elements of life threaten our wellbeing. The best personification character I could imagine for this aspect of love, was the quartermaster.

The quartermaster, or QM, is the person in the military who provides stores, equipment and weaponry. I initially imaged, based on the military significance of the role, this sonnet would largely be about battling others – fighting those whose agendas threaten us directly and intentionally. But, as I wrote the sonnet, I realised we face many different challenges in life. It would be distortive to suggest that most of our struggles are created by dedicated opponents.

So, this quartermaster is more of an expedition QM. Yes, there will be affrays that require armour and weaponry; there will also be struggles that are more akin to weathering storms and scaling indifferent cliffs.

Trust Quartermaster Love

Trust Quartermaster Love to equip you
  For storms unbrewed, for whirlwinds yet unformed,
For seismic shifts, eruptions that ensue;
Unleashing anger where rare springs once warmed.
Fast-changing nature's not your only foe,
Marauders will emerge from muddled mists;
Turncoat tormenters who approach tiptoe
Then launch themselves fleet-foot with studded fists.
Yet more than hail and hate can knock you down.
QM provides the cord to haul you up:
Geppetto threads that flip a sad soul's frown,
Olympus rope so you can nectar sup.
        Across life's span 'twixt abutments of night
        Love prepares you for each unforeseen fight.

Shakespeare had a penchant for stating things by asserting the opposite is untrue. "Love is not love that alteration finds", "Love alters not" and "Love's not Time's fool" are all taken from Sonnet 116 'Let me not to the marriage of true minds admit impediments'.

It is a powerful technique because it distinctly asserts a condition. This technique is called Litotes. In 'The Elements of Eloquence' Mark Forsyth defines Litotes as, "Affirming something by denying the opposite."

The seed idea for this personification sonnet was that love is the thing that separates us from other animals. (There are plenty of other pretenders to this throne: self-awareness, faith, language, morality. To name but a few.) However, for me, love is the key fundamental force that defines the human condition; it has the power to elevate, enhance and devastate our lives.

It is clear to me that the power to love comes from within. It is not distributed by an inhuman entity. God therefore is not love. Love is the internal power that allows us to transcend the physical experience of life.

Love's not from God

G od is not Love; no deity set out
Before tocks ticked or light blazed out of stars
With visions of a flood to quench the drought
Of hardened human hearts held behind bars.
The preacher's gambit's flipped, for Love is God:
Diviner who from matter springs forth joy,
Herald whose wings can lift each step that's trod,
Conductor whose fierce bolts will Hate destroy.
Love does not radiate from sacred shells
Dropped by celestial birds for greater good
With pow'r to alter primitive brain cells
Or expel naturists from Haven Wood.
      The old lie "God is Love" is the reverse;
      Love comes from us and shapes our universe.

1 sonnet = 14 lines. To give this project mathematical synergy, I'm writing four collections of 14 sonnets. 1 year = 52 weeks. 4 x 14 = 56. This is the mathematical truth behind my year-long Love's Sonnets project. It will, in fact, last one year and four weeks.

Furthermore, because several types of sonnet are capped with a rhyming couplet, the final two sonnets of each of my collections will function, in some way, as a pair. This week's sonnet is the first of the capping couplet pair of my initial collection 'Personification'.

In order to concoct a pair, I needed a thematic connection. Fortunately, humankind has done the thinking for me – twins. But which twins should I personify as love? Romulus and Remus fit my penchant for Classical mythology, so I went with them.

This sonnet personifies love as the less famous brother; the one who didn't found a city called Reme. The sonnet, while describing qualities and features of love, alludes to several aspects of Remus' life: born one of a twin; floated down the Tiber by someone not cruel enough to drown him; suckled by a wolf; fought alongside his brother; jumped over his brother's wall; murdered by that very same sibling.

Love is Remus

We're born with Love, the half that makes us whole
Companion when it seems that we might drown.
Love is our bosom buddy; feeds our soul
Makes common folk feel royal. It's the crown.
Love stands behind us when we need to fight,
It tears through troubles with its eagle beak;
Then on its wings lifts us up to a height
So we can see the sanctuary we seek.
Love is Remus, the part we sacrifice
When walls we've built to keep suitors at bay
Are unable to shield us from the slice
That severs to the heart and makes us prey.
   Love like Remus reflects what is inside;
   But if it shows weakness earns fratricide.

'Love's Romulus' is the fourteenth and final of my personification collection: it is partner sonnet to last week's 'Love is Remus'. This time Love is the other brother – the one who killed his twin after the cheeky sibling jumped over a wall he was building around Palatine Hill. (Having previously saved that very brother from the cruel clutches of their great uncle… who he also killed.)

Romulus was a shepherd before he was the warrior king who founded Rome. In 'Love's Romulus', I blend the ability of love to nurture and guide (the shepherd) with the characteristics of love to defend and attack. All-conquering love might sometimes seem appropriate for winning the affections we desire. But warriors become accustomed to winning with force. They are "double-edged" weapons – as capable of hurting compatriots as they are enemies.

Those raised by wolves are generally wolves.

Love's Romulus

Love's Romulus; shepherd and conqueror:
Scout when your soul must see who's on your side,
Bright beacon for the lowland wanderer,
Then god of war when interests collide.
Young Remus Love's launch is a flimsy craft
Whose naked hopes on swollen breasts fast feast,
Till strong hands grasp the crook, or keen spear's shaft;
To direct passions or repel a beast.
But like all swords, this Love is double-edged
The blade that floors the foe can flay the friend.
No eaglet mourns its down when it has fledged,
The knife that cuts the cord can too life end.

      Yes milk of lupine kindness turns love fierce
      But talons trained for war can true hearts pierce.

Forms of Love collection

The Ancient Greeks had at least six different words for love. Arguably plenty more if you include variants and subcategories.

That makes sense doesn't it? How can one word define the myriad of feelings towards our partner, children, parents, country, hobbies, food, selves etc.?

Each sonnet in this collection is inspired by a Greek or Roman word for a form of love. The form of love being explored in each sonnet is presented underneath the title.

It's ridiculous that there's only one word for love: there are clearly many different forms of this emotion, all with different strengths and effects. The Ancient Greeks had a solution – different words for different types of love. Their list included mania (obsessive love), pragma (longstanding love) and eros (sexual love). Although the length of this list is debated, most commentators agree there are at least six and that some of these can be further subdivided.

Inspired by this philosophical and pragmatic approach, my second collection of love sonnets will explore different forms of love.

This collection begins with 'Pro Patria', a sonnet exploring love of one's country. The Greeks categorised this love as a form of 'storge': this is the love you feel for family members, friends, your country or a sport team.

Pro Patria

storgē / patriotism

B eware the king who claims to be your kin;
　The general whose men's blood is empire's oil;
The fair-ground lawyer who makes senses spin.
Dyes on a map do not colour the soil.
Göring revealed the puppet master's strings:
The forward cord tugged by threats of attack,
The yellow back-line stained with shame it brings,
Grave need for front twine tight and rear thread slack.
But 'patriot' means 'fellow countryman' –
Who profits more from solidarity,
Who should ignore the false flag furtive plan
Of greedy leaders urging enmity.
　　　"Pro patria," should make us reach for blades
　　　For setting in the plough, so hunger fades.

My interest in the Ancient Greek names for love was piqued by the contrast between the single word for this emotion in English and the several names for it in Greek. There are clearly many forms of love. So why is there only one word to denote multiple emotions? Or at least multiple flavours of a single emotion?

If we use the word 'love' to describe how we feel about our partners, children, parents, jobs, hobby etc., then logic insists those interests are competing for primacy. Either actively or passively. And what human behaviour is analogous to this type of tussle? A civil war.

In this sonnet, I depict true love as the pinnacle emotion – the strongest love a person can feel. A discombobulated person's passions compete for the crown (used here as a metonym). And, as history demonstrates, there can only be one "king" in possession of a nation's regalia.

Uncivil Love

agōn / conflict

L ove is a civil war on many fronts
Ten thousand chieftains fighting for the crown
A lifelong war of sieges, frays and hunts
Ascendance gained by bringing others down.
Only one hand can wear the precious ring
Only one fist can grip the sceptre gold
One torc, one cloak, one crook made for the king
One seal to stamp dominion manifold.
Best friend, great job, cool sport, contenders are,
So too are children, parents, addiction.
They clamour with your partner for the star:
Bright guiding light of love's jurisdiction.
  To all those hurt when they're not most adored;
  The state is chaos when there is no lord.

This sonnet explores unrealised love – love that is felt emotionally but never physically. The metaphor I've created to represent this form of love is a "wildflower walk": this is a journey, on foot, to collect wild flowers for a posy.

The speaker recounts the story of such a walk, adding that they avoided plucking some "blooms" because they are "too keen to be cut off from roots" or "too proud". I add colour with specific British wild flowers, each one representing a human attitude or disposition.

In the capping couplet, the speaker explains that, as they "admire" the bunch of flowers they have collected, their "mind drifts" to those unplucked blooms.

Wildflower Walk

philía / unrealised love

M y wildflower walk encompassed fields festooned
With cups and poppies of a lucid dream,
I followed brooks, encountered briers that wound…
My quest to clasp a bunch of blooms supreme.
But buds I saw too vibrant for my home:
Some glared too keen to be cut off from roots
Some stood too proud to pull from musty loam;
Too precious for an oaf with tarnished boots.
Lone daffodil rising above the crowd,
Pink foxglove whose joy shames the hedgerow green,
Sure pimpernel as red as horns are loud,
Sharp cornflower crown fit for a faery queen,
        As I admire cut blossoms in my vase,
        My mind drifts to those bright, abandoned stars.

This 'Forms of Love' sonnet focuses on epithumia/epithumeō (desire); specifically, the desire for material things.

Nietzsche announced the "death of god" in 1882. He followed this announcement with a series of questions, one of which was, "How shall we comfort ourselves, the murderers of all murderers?" Well, the answer was already forming in the nineteenth century – consumerism. Today, most people are converts: we fill the void of religious purpose with the desire to own the latest electronic goods, vehicles, fashions and trinkets.

And, over the last century or so, as the pace of technological development has increased, we've bought into built-in obsolescence. Why repair the outdated when you can own the new?

Fellowship

epithumeō / desire

G od's coffin has been smothered with landfill;
Rank refuse of the generations who
Exchanged sweet-smelling scent for the bright pill
Of lives judged by possessions folk accrue.
Consumers saw faithful with empty hands
Clasped tight round wishful prayers as temples grew,
While shopkeepers gave joy to merry bands
Kept hooked on debt and want by trinkets new.
The weight of waste will God's corpse fossilise
Leaving a frame contorted with regret
That needy palms waved at unyielding skies
Were not with manna more routinely met.
But gods and goods both false solutions are;
For rich lives, fellowship must be the star.

This 'Forms of Love' sonnet is dedicated to the Ancient Greek 'philautía', which is love of the self. Alternatively, 'philautía' could be described as regard for your own advantage or happiness. This quality is critical; it provides us with the ability to enjoy existence.

Philautia is a life-saving medicine: too little and you perish because the dose is inadequate, too much and you die of an overdose. Insufficient self-love can lead to low self-esteem, depression, self-harm, vulnerability. Overabundance is narcissism.

A balance must therefore be struck and the perfect metaphor for this balancing act... is the "balance beam".

'Balance Beam' depicts 'philautía' as a gymnastic performance on that beam. Failing to maintain the right balance results in a fall "down one side" or "the other".

Balance Beam

philautía / self love

Self-love's gymnastics on a balance beam:
Too little and you plummet down one side,
Collapsing down the other harms the team.
To beam, or not to beam… one must decide.
Committed gymnasts judge their every move
A twist- or tumble-trip could end the act,
And yet the lively spirit yearns to prove
Its routine is failsafe, its step exact.
Side safety mats are skins on sinking sand
False promises that tested bear no weight
Quag flotsam masquerading as sound land,
Whose fickle nature fallers learn too late.
>Although maintaining balance is a fight
>The beam is the high ground, and height is right.

The Greek word that inspired this sonnet is mania… obsessive love.

The metaphors for the love interest in each quatrain develop through the sonnet. At first, the object of affection / adoration / obsession is a "flare" shot into the sky by a person in distress.

In the second quatrain, the love interest is golden treasure "buried deep" underground. The speaker's claim to be able to "cleanse" its golden "spirit", suggests they feel moral superiority over their acquisition.

In the final quatrain, the love interest is a "coloured diamond" that has been "won" by the speaker. In this quatrain, the relationship between speaker and love interest has become one of ownership: the "flaws" within their form become the means of controlling them.

The capping couplet sums up the relationship between speaker and the person who has inspired their mania. The object of interest has become exactly that – an object.

Flare

mania / controlling obsessive love

Your face a flare; the crowd dull huddled clouds
Transcended by the beacon bold and bright
That these grey ghouls would smother with their shrouds
Before your glow can set the scene alight.
Your spirit gold: precious and buried deep.
Keen hunter, I will prize you from your cell.
My shining cloth will mop the tears you weep,
And cleanse you of that subterranean hell.
Your form, cut coloured diamond in my hand
At auction won by my impressive bid,
Your unique flaws are sure as any brand,
A treasure simply traced need not be hid.
  When I have glimpsed a chance, I grab the grail,
  No storm, no spoil, no price, will make me fail.

'Survival', like many of my sonnets, arranges clauses in atypical orders. Poetic licence presents the opportunity to arrange clauses in ways that would seem incorrect in prose. For example, in the first quatrain, the speaker will "suffocate" with the "awful weight" of the "absence" of their desire's love. But instead of using following the prosaic convention of arranging this thought in logical order (I will suffocate without your love), this thought is peppered throughout the quatrain.

In the second quatrain, the speaker declares they will "die of thirst" in the first line. The object of this 'sentence' is presented in the fourth line of the quatrain: "without the source of you".

Arranging clauses in atypical orders, and threading meaning throughout compound and complexes sentences, can befuddle. It can make it more difficult to decipher meaning. In the week when I was sad to hear of the passing of Meat Loaf, a stalwart of my teenage discos, he was very clear about what he would not do "for love". In 1998, Meat Loaf told VH1 the confusion over this phrase came from a misunderstanding of the structure of the song. The answer was there all along… appearing two lines earlier than the line "but I won't do that", every time he sang it.

Survival

mania / dependent obsessive love

You are the air I breathe, I'll suffocate
Lungs veined with pain as if in acid dipped
Chest crushed by you vacuum, the awful weight
Of your absence leaving lone me blue-lipped.
You are my eau-de-vie, I'll die of thirst
Lips slashed as if by imps with vicious knives
Light head like a grenade about to burst
Without the source of you that me revives.
You are my sustenance, my fuel wellspring,
I weaken quick, my limbs turn limp as foam
My stomach screams as hunger hornets sting
When you empty the cupboards of my home.
      I'll suffocate, thirst, starve without your near
      Losing your life support's my greatest fear.

This 'Forms of Love' sonnet is dedicated to the Ancient Greek 'pragma': enduring love.

If Love is enduring, it remains strong over time. It is therefore in competition with time. This thought led to the idea of writing a sonnet in which Time (personified) attacks Love.

The fist quatrain depicts Time as both "vandal" defacing a monument and "mollusc" leaving trails on it. The second quatrain has Time as the creator of a chemical weapon; the third presents Time as a "tempest" smashing "incessant waves" onto the deck of "pleasure craft" Love.

The capping couplet declares Love's victory over Time. Time does not diminish Love, it enriches it.

Time v Love

prâgma / enduring love

Time targets Love with chisels and with nails:
A vandal gouging grooves into smooth stone,
Dull mollusc leaving slow-appearing trails –
Wounds though they seem skin-deep cut to the bone.
Time taints the air we breathe with toxicants
That bloat the limbs, turn faces into masks
Of gargoyles gross chewing on wasps and ants
And swigging vinegar from mouldy casks.
Time is a tempest; Love a pleasure craft
That creaks and groans under incessant waves
Of weeks and hours smashing fore and aft
Hell-bent to send the crew to early graves.
    Yet Love's no lost pilgrim in search of cures,
    As years pass by, like whiskey, it matures.

My poetic exploration of Ancient Greek words for love continues this week with a focus on ludus: playful love. (Which is actually a Roman concept.) Ludus is the experience of young lovers: having a crush, teasing, dancing and flirting. (It's not a board game with four differently coloured quadrants – that's Ludo.)

'Playful Love' is arranged in three quatrains with a capping couplet. The first quatrain depicts playful love in its infancy; the second features middle-aged love; the third has elderly love "mummified".

The capping couplet delivers the resolution: if love is allowed to play regularly, it stays youthful.

Let's Play

lūdus / playful love

L ove is a childish game: it's hide and seek,
It's kiss-chase playgrounds buzzed with playful screams
It's pillow fighting as bounced bed springs squeak
It's dressing up, exploring adult themes.
In middle age the games become constrained
The skipping stops, the giggling gears cease up
The reservoir of joy is slowly drained
The old dog growls annoyance at the pup.
And at its end playful Love's mummified:
Its dehydrated heart a raisin shrunk,
Belief that life is fun a dream that's died,
The hope-launched party boat a ship that's sunk.
   But unlike flesh, Love ages not with days
   It stays forever young if oft it plays.

This week's 'Forms of Love' sonnet is inspired by the Ancient Greek word 'φιλία/philía': affectionate regard or friendship. It is love without physical attraction. Plato did not see physical attraction as a necessary part of love. For this reason, philía is commonly known as Platonic love.

'Repression Alchemy' is the launch pad for my exploration of philía. It focuses on the effect of *not* entering into an intimate relationship with someone.

The metaphor for this experience is the child's "toy" left inside its original packaging. Although I've personally found it ridiculous that an untouched toy is worth far more than one that has been loved and played with, this poem presents the logic of the collector who desires untarnished playthings.

Repression Alchemy

philía / friendship

I struggled to believe them when they claimed
  A toy is worth more left inside the box;
The cradle-coffin by designers aimed
To be as popular as chicken pox.
Restraint they urged / denial of the self:
Pretend that feel and fun are valueless,
Enjoy not games, place playthings on a shelf,
Push not the train, do not the doll undress.
For them, a tactile act is blasphemy
Contact infects knickknacks with seeping sores.
Rather they urge repression alchemy;
The gifts that turn to gold stay in the drawers.
        I thought them speculators, cash-obsessed,
        Now know you should not maul what you love best.

This week I continue to explore φιλία/philía' (affectionate regard or friendship). Last week's sonnet depicted platonic love as love that benefits from restraint – from not becoming tainted by carnal intimacy. This time I celebrate friendship that is entirely separate from any form of romantic or erotic desire: true friendship.

This week I've formed two polyptotons: "repeated use of one word as different parts of speech or in different grammatical forms". The first, in line one, is "Friend" as a proper noun and "friendship" as an abstract noun; a proper noun you can feel with your fingers, an abstract noun you feel with your heart.

The second polyptoton is "Firm" and "firma". Although these both have the same meaning, one is an adjective in common use whereas the other is half of a common noun in uncommon use.

Dear Friend

philía / friendship

Dear Friend, your friendship is a love most true;
It's not a fire ignited when a match
Is struck to kindle passions red and blue:
Bold flames that will Lust's jet fuel fast despatch.
Our friendly love is rooted in the earth
Rich placenta of Mother Nature's womb
Firm terra firma whose bountiful worth
Is brought to light when flora starts to bloom.
It flexes like a willow when storms strike
As ivy to foundations it clings tight.
We're mutually supportive, we both like
To see each other flourish in the light.
    Love's not a bugle signal to retreat;
    It's music that resounds when we friends meet.

Storge. Familial love. The first sonnet of this collection was dedicated to one expression of this form of love: patriotism. This week's is dedicated to the essence of all patriotism: family love. The strongest bond of all.

It can be hard to maintain familial love. Partners aside, we don't choose our family members. This sonnet reflects that reality by presenting both sides of the story. Some appreciate these "vital" connections; some feel the need to free themselves of genetic "manacles".

Blood Bonds

storgē / familial love

The bonds of blood for some are vital veins
  That join disjointed forms through thick and thin;
When birth's cord's cut they're the twine that remains
Connecting new born hope to loving kin.
For some, the bonds of blood are manacles
Nailed to the wall of a dank dungeon cell
Each link an iron-rich round corpuscle
That ties them to their bleak ancestral hell.
Blood can be buried but can't be denied,
It forms the mould in which our lives are cast.
Blood is a knot that cannot be untied
Nor cut. It stays fast as Time marches past.
          If your bloody connections threaten pain
          Could they somehow be fixed to work again?

This 'forms of love' sonnet is inspired by pragma: enduring love. The opposite of enduring love is short-term selfishness.

This sonnet makes the case for pragma by presenting a grasping, flawed argument for short-term selfishness. The theme throughout the three quatrains is the need for stuff: fire, air, water and earth. (These were the pre-Socratic basic elements.)

The speaker argues for their need for these elements. In the first quatrain they state their needs. In the second quatrain they consider others' desire for the same resources. In the third quatrain they ask why they should share them.

The capping couplet presents the counterargument. Love. Greedy people feed themselves with stuff… but starve themselves of love.

Elements of Desire

prâgma / enduring love

I am a fire who needs fuel to survive,
I am a ship that sails Time's stormy seas,
A waterfall that roars to feel alive,
A rigid oak stood proud of other trees.
Yes there are other flames in need of wax
Other schooners with rigging tough and sound
A myriad of bright streams making tracks
A forest of tall trees fixed to the ground.
Why should I share the oil in short supply?
Why should I share the winds that bloat my sails?
I need a flood to sing a lullaby
Without a mass of earth my grand trunk fails.
  Logic suggests I should grasp all I need
  But Love love's empathy and abhors greed.

The final sonnet of my 'Forms of Love' collection is dedicated to agápē or selfless love.

"Greater love hath no man than this, that a man lay down his life for his friends." – John15:13.

(And I quote the bible as an atheist who recognises enduring wisdom.)

To Others

agápē / sacrificial love

I could not live the life I love without
Your sacrifice. I could not be the me
I am if you'd not ceased to be. Yet doubt
You thought of me when you fought to be free.
Nor could you know fresh faces yet unformed –
Preoccupied in land once occupied,
Untroubled by the threat that your world stormed,
Living fulfilling lives because you died.
Though battlefields are littered with regrets
No soldier croaks wishing they had not tried
To carry on their ironed epaulettes
The hopes of civil folk their country wide.

Your selfless love is generations long
There is no gift as great, no bond so strong.

(from As You Like It, spoken by Jaques)

All the world's a stage,
And all the men and women merely players;
They have their exits and their entrances;
And one man in his time plays many parts,
His acts being seven ages. At first the **infant**,
Mewling and puking in the nurse's arms;
And then the whining **school-boy**, with his satchel
And shining morning face, creeping like snail
Unwillingly to school. And then the **lover**,
Sighing like furnace, with a woeful ballad
Made to his mistress' eyebrow. Then a **soldier**,
Full of strange oaths, and bearded like the pard,
Jealous in honour, sudden and quick in quarrel,
Seeking the bubble reputation
Even in the cannon's mouth. And then the **justice**,
In fair round belly with good capon lin'd,
With eyes severe and beard of formal cut,
Full of wise saws and modern instances;
And so he plays his part. The **sixth age** shifts
Into the lean and slipper'd pantaloon,
With spectacles on nose and pouch on side;
His youthful hose, well sav'd, a world too wide
For his shrunk shank; and his big manly voice,
Turning again toward childish treble, pipes
And whistles in his sound. Last scene of all,
That ends this strange eventful history,
Is **second childishness** and mere oblivion;
Sans teeth, sans eyes, sans taste, sans everything.

- Willm Shakp

Ages & Sins collection

This third collection combines the logic of maths with the playfulness of creative writing and canonical nature of literary history.

14 is comprised of two sevens → there are two well-established sevens in the English literary cannon (Shakespeare's Seven Ages of Man and the Desert Fathers' Seven Deadly Sins) → this collection combines these two famous sevens.

Sonnets 29 – 35 respond to the "seven ages"; sonnets 36 – 42 are inspired by the seven deadly sins (set out in traditional order).

The Ages will come first. Shakespeare's first age is the infant, "Mewling and puking in the nurse's arms". This sonnet is therefore an exploration of infant life.

As throughout this project, love is the focus. However, the noun "love" does not appear until the final couplet. It doesn't need to. Every preceding illustration of an infant's experience is bursting with love.

This delayed appearance of "love" gives the capping couplet greater conclusive power. The focus changes from examples of love in early life to the importance of it. Infants raised with love are more likely to be able to cope with the "heights" and "lows" they experience in later life.

Infant Love

The infant's first intake of breath declares
  Their independence from the bass drum beat
That pounded through the chest of she who bears
The task of forming trembling hands and feet.
The infant's first bold-apprehensive step
Shows confidence and vulnerability;
Stage one of life's long unrelenting schlep
Through storms that threaten keen stability.
When first the infant speaks the world prepares
For the lid to be lifted off the jar
That seals inside wants, needs, fears, hopes and cares
That unleashed spread trapped thoughts to realms afar.
      If love is added as the small child grows,
      They'll learn to savour heights and cope with lows.

The second stage in Shakespeare's "seven ages" of man is the "schoolboy". Throughout my Love's Sonnets series, I've attempted to make the 'lover' as gender neutral as possible so anyone can imagine they are the subject of each poem. Therefore, in this sonnet, we have the "schoolchild" rather than "schoolboy".

As they progress through their school years, most schoolchildren mature from loving their parents or carers above all others... to loving others more than their parents or carers. During this process, they are pulled in two different directions. This sonnet portrays that transition as a "sailor" dangling between a "jetty" (parental figures) and a departing "ship" (a lover). As the ship heads out to sea, the sailor needs to decide which to hold on to.

The penalty for not making the decision (to either remain within the family bosom or explore foreign lands) is plunging into the cold harbour and spending your life lonely and sad "with a cold and salty face".

The Schoolchild's Love

The schoolchild's love's a sailor gripping tight
To jetty and to slow-departing ship:
Firm wharf's the land that nurtured mind and might,
Wild craft's the promise of a thrilling trip.
The sounder choice might seem to be the shore
Safe solid motherland (both seed and soil)
That does not shift or shake at Neptune's roar
And will not sink, nor from tempests recoil.
But bedecked vessel flies flags flittering
That signal fun, frolics and fantasies
As it leaves portly town folk twittering –
A flock of homing pigeons on the quays.
      By school's last bell the child must choose one base,
      Or live life with a cold and salty face.

This is the third of seven sonnets based on Shakespeare's "Seven Ages of Man": "the lover".

Shakespeare has his lover "sighing like furnace"; a forlorn figure writing "a woeful ballad". I've created a more positive young lover – someone whose "racing heart" is set off by the "Starting Pistol" of a "track" race.

This young "lover's love" explodes into action;
their goal is to reach the finish line "tape" that must be crossed before they can access their beloved's "treasured face".

Starting Pistol

The lover's love is set off by the gun
　Of the official standing at the start
Holding a pistol fiery as the sun
Whose single shot begins the racing heart
That sets jet aircraft speeding through the veins
With oxygen for muscles to consume
That turn the lover's legs to bullet trains
So round the track, a Bolt, young love can zoom
Towards the tape that marks the finish line –
The single-minded focus of its race
The final fence of Aphrodite's shrine
The gateway to their idol's treasured face.
　　　Young love, once triggered, knows not how to walk
　　　It might look like a dove; but it's a hawk.

The weekly sonnets continue with the fourth of Shakespeare's "seven ages" of man... the soldier.

A soldier's drive to fight is strongly connected to love of country and love of fellow citizens. That love must be very strong if they are willing to risk life and limb for it.

This sonnet compares a "soldier's love" to that of a "lover". Both are a fire, but the soldier's must be "fiercer" because of the risks the soldier takes. The motif of "fire" is threaded through the poem. Regular alliteration of "f" alludes to flickering flames. The capping couplet concludes with juxtaposed metaphors of "cold" and "warm" blood.

The Soldier's Love

The soldier's love is fiercer than the fire
Of two dry bushes set off with a flash;
The heat of battle's hotter than desire
Which flickers fleetingly then turns to ash.
Each lover loves a handful in their time
While fighters love the millions of their land;
The lover lies in bed while church clocks chime
As soldiers fall face first on earth and sand.
Though passion may the heart a skipping send,
Set lips and organs tingling with delight:
No kisses can a broken body mend,
No tender hug will end a firefight.
Think not a soldier's blood runs thin and cold
That blood, when spilt, runs rich, and warm, and bold.

This sonnet explores the perspective of the "justice" from Shakespeare's "seven ages of man". Although this project is dedicated to love, to judge is the opposite of loving. To judge or not to judge, that is the question.

This sonnet therefore pits judge against lover. These characters represent opposing viewpoints. The lover enjoys "foibles" whereas the judge "Delights in errors". The lover looks for the good in someone, the judge seeks out the "flaws". Shakespeare's "justice" has "eyes severe", after all.

I've liberally employed alliteration. The internal rhyme of "While" with "bile" and "smile" enhances the impact of the eleventh line. I use repetition in line six to aurally represent the movement of a performer. And the theatrical setting reflects the established relationship between poetry and theatre.

Judging

To love or judge, the punter must decide
  When a fresh player tumbles into view
On a round stage where there's no place to hide
Whose tricks, costume and face are fancies new.
The judge measures the act with sniper's eye
Each turn, each step, each leap precisely weighed;
The self-same strides will make the lover cry
They sense intent in every move that's made.
The judge searches for flaws to feed their bile,
Delights in errors – trips – so they can scorn;
While quirks and foibles curl the lover's smile
Who loves the fancy rose despite its thorn.
        You cannot have two hearts: lover and judge;
        What will you bring to fling, flowers or sludge?

This sonnet explores the significance of love during Shakespeare's "sixth age". It is a response to the negative connotations in Jaques' famous "All the world's a stage" monologue. The themes of a "shrunk shrank", "whistles" in the voice and "spectacles on nose" are positively interpreted.

The first quatrain uses repeated prolepsis (the use of a descriptive word in anticipation of it becoming applicable). Several examples of "it" are given without an explanation of what "it" is. This is revealed with the first word of the second quatrain "Love". Love is followed with a full stop to create a pause for reflection: caesura.

Other linguistic techniques include onomatopoeia "beats bold"; which is also alliterative as is "Love. Like a lava" and "beam … buttress … brace". There are several similes using "like" to draw comparison plus metaphors to illustrate the structural importance of grandparents' love.

Sixth Sense

Time makes it stronger like maturing cheese;
Like wine or whiskey it improves with age;
Like Roman concrete mixed for salty quays
It becomes surer as the years' waves rage:
Love. Like a lava island bigger grows,
So when the shank of the sixth age is shrunk
The child who holds the grandparent's hand knows
The heart beats bold inside the ageing trunk.
The whistle in the voice is the love song –
The trilling of the wren on autumn eves;
The glasses on the nose make focus strong
To help see dreams that the grandchild believes.
　　　The sixth age fortifies the human race
　　　It is the beam, the buttress and the brace.

In my final response to Shakespeare's 'seven ages' of man, this sonnet rejects the suggestion that decline in old age is "mere oblivion". In a society that treasures "expressions of perfection", it's not surprising that we "shun" old age and cognitive decline.

However, my capping couplet attests, that if Shakespeare's "second childishness" is akin to that of the "infant", then logic suggests we should love the "elder" of the two in equal measure.

As the final sonnet of this collection, the title forms a pair with the penultimate 'Sixth Sense'. This caps off my 'seven ages' demi-collection. In the second half of this collection of 14 sonnets, I will explore the relationship between love and the seven deadly sins.

Sans Sense

The seventh age is noted for what's sans
As sense and senses melt like candle wax:
We take for granted what's good till it's gone
The frozen pond's a playground till it cracks.
To never have's an aching, nagging pain
A burden borne, an unremitting cost;
To lose what's had is piercing needle rain
That pricks parts of the brain that feel what's lost.
Who would not wish to stroke de Milo's arms?
Or sail beneath Colossus in the sun?
Expressions of perfection have their charms
While decay and decline do oglers shun.
       But if the infant's loved for childishness
       Why should we love the elder any less?

Onto the second half of my 'Ages and Sins' collection…
the seven deadly sins.

According to my research, there is a generally accepted order:
pride (or vainglory), greed, or covetousness, lust, envy,
gluttony (which also includes drunkenness), wrath or anger,
and sloth. So I'll write a love-related sonnet in response
to each sin, in that order.

The sins were deemed such in Medieval times because they
were examples of people putting their own interests before
those of God. Gluttony, for example, is the love of food and
drink that, if taken to excess, supplants the required primacy
of the love of God. As a committed atheist, I don't plan
to dwell on the theological aspect of the sins for the whole
collection. But I have deemed it necessary to do so in the first.

Pride

To love your strengths, they say, demeans their God:
  Denies their hungry Lord the love he needs,
Clangs discord through that loyal, cloistered squad –
Frightened the Power might fade that on love feeds.
Love's not a bottle stuck up on a shelf
Slow-emptied with each shot of spirit sunk:
It's a wellspring set deep inside the self
That flows full fast despite how much is drunk.
Why would a God determine to deny
The air balloon that rises as it swells?
Unless that higher power hogs the sky
So he can look down on love-emptied shells.
        If being proud of good things is a sin,
        Then good's not good, and there's no God within.

This is the first Love's Sonnet sonnet to have contemporary (ish) quotes: "Greed is good" and "Loadsa money". Both lines were intended to criticise the greed culture of the 1980s: both ended up being the celebrated catchphrases of those they intended to lambast.

The problem with trying to impose a moral perspective is those who are "ardent" believers of the opposite position, will use their "hardened shell" to protect themselves from criticism. In this sonnet, I acknowledge that reality.

If I wanted to encourage the greedy to change their ways, my attempts to redirect them would be far less effective than those of much greater "writers". In fact, even stood on someone's "shoulders", a placard held by me would not be seen above the metaphorical "shoes" of such writers.

I therefore, at the end, advise critics to stop sounding warnings. (But, between you and me, I hope acknowledging it is the responsibility of the individual to recognise and manage their own greed, might be the more effective strategy for affecting change.)

Greed

That "Greed is good" was meant to be critique
And "Loadsa money" written to repel;
But direct lines can quickly turn oblique
When they impact an ardent's hardened shell.
Beware the unintended consequence
Of cautions hung to terrify the soul;
All Dickens' ghouls, regardless of their tense
Were clear in message, consequence and goal.
If I stood on the shoulders of my muse
With placard calling for greed to be 'STOPPED!'
My message would not rise above the shoes
Of mighty writers whose warnings have flopped.
Consumers won't be told consumption's wrong
So critics: mute the bell and melt the gong.

Pure lust, like pure alcohol, is dangerous. But alcohol-free gin is just flavoured water… selling for £30 a bottle! If I want invigorating water, I'll stick my face in a cascading mountain stream.

Is lust an acceptable aspect of love? Each quatrain of this sonnet explores a different side of the argument: lustless love is "limp"; loveless lust is "violent"; a mix is needed.

The third quatrain is influenced by Shakespeare's Sonnet 116. The Bard uses himself to justify his argument in 116, "If this be error and upon me proved, / I never writ, nor no man ever loved." In tribute to dead Bill, my sonnet suggests a burette (a precise measuring device used in chemistry whose name derives from an ecclesiastic jug) is needed to "acc'rately" mix love and lust.

Lust

Love without lust's a lonely lettuce leaf
Unfingered in a fridge: cold, limp and grim;
Ignored by carnivores who fancy beef,
And gastronomes seeking vigour and vim.
But lust sans love's a stalker's bugle call,
A seed that can sprout violent purple blooms,
The looter who cares only for their haul,
The gleeful thief who desecrates sealed tombs.
A mix of these two potent potions must
Solution be to keep passion alive;
To get it right the clever chemist must
Find a burette that can measures contrive.
      Without the means to balance acc'rately
      We're beasts unfit to crawl out of the sea.

Exploring love through the lens of the seven deadly sins has compelled me to justify them. Each sin is, after all, overwhelming love for something. The sins are meant to be avoided because they are manifestations of people loving things more than they love god.

I'm happy to argue for them. I actively promote loving anything and everything above that of an imaginary, narcissistic, cruel dictator.

Each quatrain of this sonnet explores a different form of envy: wealth, skill, power. The consistent suggestion is that there is no valid reason for accepting disproportionate ownership of any of these qualities.

The capping couplet concludes the argument: "others" don't want the masses to be envious... because that threatens their stranglehold.

Envy

Why should I love not what the rich have got?
  To possess they have comrades dispossessed,
Or hoarded common goods to brim their pot
While empty stomachs howl like wolves possessed.
If it is skills why can't I emulate?
The untrained is the victim in a duel,
The greatest epithet is to be Great,
Heroes ambrosia gulp, losers sip gruel.
Why should the poor not envy power held
In taloned fists of megalomaniacs?
The cruel master's watchtower must be felled;
The natural successor wields the axe.
        It's those with vaults who spread the septic lie
        That envy weighs down those to wish to fly.

Gluttony. Excessive eating and drinking. This fifth sonnet of my seven deadly sins collection, marks 5/7 of the way through my project to write a sonnet every week for a year.

This sonnet is a celebration of gluttony. I have used synaesthesia (the rhetorical technique of describing one sense in terms of another) to construct a celebration of consumption.

This jovial cross-sensory allusion is enhanced by puns: "Trumpet mushrooms", "rich … cream horn; "lemon[-]cello", "champagne flutes". Many of my sonnets to date have been somewhat earnest; it was fun to be lighthearted for a change.

The capping couplet uses the playful sound of a "swanee whistle" (a noise sometimes used to lampoon obesity) to euphemistically dismiss criticisms of a contented glutton.

Gluttony

I eat a symphony of sour and sweet:
Discordant snacks – musicians tuning up,
Conductor's baton sets my heart's quick beat,
My stomach mumbles as the room fills up.
The drawl of violins – apéritif
The zingling bell tree is a piquant soup
Trumpet mushrooms herald carpaccio beef
And snare drum scallops send me cock-a-hoop.
The strings combined – gravy by angels kissed
Next rasping rich bass tones of the cream horn
Cleansed by the limoncello soloist
Then cheerful champagne flutes prattling till morn.
     I savour every note, both sharp and flat;
     Give not a swanee whistle that I'm fat.

In making the case for anger, I needed to understand how it benefits us. Chatting to my wife, she suggested anger protects us from forces that conspire to undermine us.

I agree.

I get angry when things threaten the essence of my being: challenges that begin to overwhelm me; hurdles I can't leap; people who compel me to sacrifice qualities I'm proud of; things I love about myself and the world around me.

Anger, therefore, is love's defender.

Anger

Is anger ostracised? Why should we not
Sup from the 'cano cup when pressure mounts?
Thrash in the thermal pool when it is hot?
With feet unto our fire, settle accounts?
Without red rage no dictators would fall
Or evil occupiers be repulsed
Or unjust laws be toppled with the wall
That warders watched bricked up as they convulsed.
Those that exploit us want anger suppressed:
It is the force that cracks the tyrant's yoke
It's the substance that swells the honest chest
The blade that cuts the bonds that would us choke.
    Our anger is the shield that lets us love –
    The eagle that drives falcons from the dove.

In my final 'seven deadly sins' sonnet (also the final sonnet in my 'Ages & Sins' collection), I make the case for sloth. As with all my musings in this miniseries, I take the position that a so-called sin is love for something that others deem unacceptable. And who would determine sloth a sin? The grafter, of course!

The speaker of this poem is self-admittedly slothful. Their "body loves to lounge", "rest" works for them, sloth "troubles" them not. The speaker addresses their antipode – providing a counterargument to challenge that hardworking critic.

The capping couplet suggests their complainant believes themselves to be more worthy – closer to god. (Sloth is a sin, after all.)

Sloth

My sloth troubles me not yet you it irks,
The fat within my skin gets under yours,
Rest works for me; for you endeavour works,
My body loves to lounge; yours pause abhors.
You place my 'free and easy' in the dock:
Who's in the right? Who has the right to judge?
A sledgehammer will smash a gavel's block
And hands moving too fast pronouncements smudge.
Your issue with my leisure is you need
Conclusive validation of your choice:
To strain and sweat, to blister and to bleed,
To volunteer your brawn, to lend your voice.
      Lord if you cannot handle my malaise…
      Begone, seek active angels you can praise.

Love Letters collection

Each of the sonnets in this collection is a letter to someone, or something, I love, or have loved.

This is the first of my fourth and final series of fourteen sonnets: Love Letters.

Each of these sonnets is a letter to someone, or something, I love, or have loved. Deeply.

I will not reveal who, or what, each letter is dedicated to.

'We River' is an extended metaphor. It begins with theft from A Midsummer Night's Dream: "The course of true love never did run smooth." The first line of the sonnet uses this logic to establish the metaphor of love as a river. It then explores the commonalities of these two nouns: one concrete, one abstract.

As always, this sonnet was not the one I imagined I'd write at the outset. Starting a poem is like tipping the pieces out of a jigsaw puzzle with no picture on the box.

We River

Love runs not smooth, it's river it's not lake:
Crash-smashing into rocks as if it can
Remove the obstacles that make it snake;
Brash barriers to water's forward plan.
But rivers have to twist, contort and writhe
Rave raucously on beds and over drops;
They're beautiful because they're wild and lithe
Their fervour races on… it never stops.
At times our liquid love reaches full flood
With pow'r to drag us down amongst the weeds;
At others it dries up like rage-spilt blood
On battlefields distressed by vicious deeds.
       But never will our river cease to move
       No damn drawback could its essence remove.

I'll keep this short because I'm on holiday with family; this collection is proving the hardest to write. I thought practising writing sonnets would have made the process easier.
But it's not the process that's hard with my Love Letters collection: it's the sentiment.

Each sonnet in this collection is a letter to someone I love, or have loved. Each one has to be sincere, appropriate, true.

'Alchemist' is about my twentieth attempt to write a poetic letter to the intended recipient. It contains the essence of some earlier versions, but is largely distinct.

It contains fewer linguistic techniques. It's simpler. That's because earlier versions with hyperbole, grand metaphors and fantastical allusions felt false. This sonnet feels true.

That will be my litmus test for this series. Art must be true: love must be true.

Alchemist

My love for you ain't easy to describe
It's a potion both potent and complex
Whose concoction no scientist could scribe
Yet blows my mind with its profound effects.
Ways that I've loved you I have had to change –
Stop-motion memories (a treasured store)
That pushy Time has forced me to exchange
For nostalgia that swells my chest yet more.
Those moments in my heart's vessel are mixed
With admiration for who you are now
A character of virtues, firmly fixed
Who rich furrows in life will surely plough
      You've mixed this past, present and future list
      And made you gold, you're your own alchemist.

Having avoided hyperbole in last week's sonnet, I've
rediscovered my affection for this linguistic technique.
This change reminds me how my mood affects my writing;
one day I might like a form of expression, another day
I might detest it. It's a poet's prerogative!

This Love Letter is dedicated to someone I admire; someone
who projects positivity. And what better metaphor for
a projector of brightness than a lighthouse? And, when
choosing a lighthouse, what reason could there be for
choosing one other than the greatest ever known?
The Lighthouse of Alexandria, also known as the Pharos
of Alexandra or just Pharos (the island on which it was built).

Beacon

I love you like moth mariners who see
The Pharos' beacon proud above dark swells
That, as they flutter near, lights up with glee
Brows scarred by biting squalls and lashing hells.
Like the lighthouse your flames will long outlast
The dreamers who laid your foundation stones
For though your blaze burns bold and fierce and fast
Your stoker spirit grafts and never moans.
You are an ardent wonder to behold:
Great as Colossus, curious as the Sphynx,
A soul more precious than a fleece of gold
Who like Athena makes. And wars. And thinks.
  Those who doubt this sonnet's sincerity
  Have never known such love. And don't know me.

An adage from my advertising days was, if you want people to catch one ball... throw them one ball. Throw them ten and they'll catch the wrong one. Or none. This axiom is as important in creative writing. A poem with several points is a roll of barbed wire; a poem with one point is an arrow. (Capable of breaking a heart, or killing a king.)

This sonnet is both an extended metaphor and an extended comparison. Other linguistic techniques are subtle. Light alliteration "gleam" & "gold" / "hear" & "hurt" / " broad" & "brave" / "fairness", "frightening" & "fragile" is threaded through the sonnet. An oxymoron draws attention to the ability of the addressee to "hear the ... mute"; caesura in line eight emboldens the sentence "You help everyone"; and an allusion in the capping couplet (to another statuesque lady) completes the metaphorical exploration.

Justice

Justice, they say, is blind to influence
Sees not the gleam of scimitar or gold
Yet she is armed to fight in the defence
Of barons who have this deception sold.
You stand for justice without a faux mask
Or need for statues to each battle won;
You hear the hurt and mute who cannot ask
For your assistance. You help anyone.
The broad brave arm you use to wield your sword
You place around the struggling and the weak:
For fairness is not frightening the horde –
It's heartening the fragile and the meek.
      I love you for the standard you hold high
      The torch you bear for others lights the sky.

Like all activities in life, some sonnets are hard graft, some flow. Those two experiences are related. Sometimes early graft provides later ease; sometimes early ease engenders later graft. I spent a long time thinking about this sonnet. The process of writing it was fluid and fast.

Rhyme appears in several forms. In addition to the Shakespearian sonnet rhyme scheme (ababcdcdefefgg) there is internal rhyme "turn … concern", "flayed … slashed", "out without"; alliteration "where … once", "black … blazed", "bright blazed", "trust … turn"; and assonance "hardened tar", "No words … comfort", "flayed … eyes", "hidden built-in". The combined effect of the congruousness of these techniques is a melodic aural tone. (I specify 'aural' to distinguish the sound of the poem from its narrative tone.)

Disappearance

I thought I was deep hurt because you'd gone
Left a black hole where once bright blazed a star;
An aching vacuum where your light had shone
Cold as deep space and dark as hardened tar.
But as time stretched I realised my pain
Was amplified because you'd left no note
No words to comfort, justify, explain
The sting that flayed my eyes and slashed my throat.
How could you leave without the slightest sign
You'd set out without ever coming back?
Did you breed trust to turn concern malign
Or wall construct with hidden built-in crack?
       The wound of your departure's never healed;
       My heart, from that cruel shock, has been annealed.

This Love Letter is an extended metaphor: it credits the addressee with having built the narrator into a giant statue, then helped them come to life. A Titan.

The first quatrain describes the "mound" and "foundations" on which a statue is to be built. The second quatrain details the process of creating a statue capable of withstanding "storms" (challenging situations). The third suggests this "monument" has been brought to life with a "heart beat" and given Mercury's "sandals" so it can move with great speed.

The capping couplet delivers the counterpunch. Although the addressee's "faith" in the narrator gave them self-belief, the absence of ongoing support has caused their collapse. This image of a "crumbled" statue alludes to another sonnet about humbling reality: 'Ozymandias'.

Moving Monument

Your open-hearted welcome was the mound
　　Raised up to give a view of vistas gold;
Your open-armed affection cleared the ground
For broad foundations that high hopes could hold.
Acceptance of my nature was the stone
On which you built the monument of me;
Endorsement of my traits the rock backbone
That let me withstand storms, meet trials carefree.
Your eulogy was gilt that made me shine,
Your love the spell that made my cold heart beat
Your songs of praise with my dreams did combine
To flying sandals strap upon my feet.
　　　　Your faith made me believe that I could soar
　　　　But since you've gone, I've crumbled to the floor.

The Shakespearian sonnet provides substantial structure: 14 lines comprised of three quatrains with a capping couplet, iambic pentameter, designated rhyme scheme, capping couplet regularly offering a riposte or summation that invites the reader to find a deeper meaning.

This sonnet has an even tighter structure; the first two lines of each quatrain present an animal with seemingly negative characteristics, the second two lines present an animal with contrasting characteristics.

The addressee is a "stubborn" "donkey", an "ass" even. They have the memory of an "elephant" and the "awkward" nature of an "orangutan". This is contrasted with dutiful animals like the "horse" that obeys commands, the "loyal" "dog" and the "caged bird" with its angelic melody.

The capping couplet encourages the reader to consider whether they want someone with "servile" qualities: it suggests such "qualities" are fickle, whereas the "fierce" love of the "unrefined" beast is far more valuable.

Stubborn Beast

You are a donkey, stubborn, unrefined
   An ass unwilling to direction change:
The horse, however, by man is designed
To turn, to charge, to halt, patrol the range.
You are an elephant that won't forget
Details that should trickle through cracks in time:
Unlike the dog, mankind's most loyal pet
Forgiving cruel owners' every crime.
You're an orangutan, awkward and loud
Your nest's a mess, food is found everywhere:
Unlike the caged bird plucked out of a cloud
Neat as a housemaid singing servile prayer.
       But fickle are the trained beast's qualities;
       While your fierce love won't flinch, won't flee, won't freeze.

In this sonnet I have used caesura to represent the "misaligned" nature of myself and the addressee. Caesura is a pause or break in a line of poetry. The word comes from the from past participle stem of the Latin 'caedere' – 'to cut'.

'Misaligned' is an extended metaphor of two bridges being built across an "estuary". But they are not destined to "meet": both construction projects are led by engineers "convinced / Their routes" are correct.

The sonnet is loaded with language that belongs to a lexical field relating to self-confidence: "earnest", "convinced", "true", "sure", "confidence", self-belief", "resolved", "assured", "right". These words are applied to both bridgebuilders.

The capping couplet reveals a truth that the speaker of the poem has waited until the end to notice… and reveal. The two engineers are not only alike in assuredness, they are also similar in "design".

Misaligned

Our bonds were bridgeheads misaligned that could
Not meet. Two earnest engineers convinced
Their routes were true: equipped with tools that would
Mark out straight paths, sure plans to be evinced.
And as our jetties jutted out into
The void, our blinkered confidence obscured
Those who the raw flaw saw. So out we grew,
Rigid in self-belief: resolved, assured.
You reached the other side; I'm not yet free
From toil. Yet glancing back, there was no way
We could connect. Our piers suggested we
Were right: critics could not our choices sway.
        But as I pause to scan the estuary,
        I see you have the same design as me.

There's a structure within the structure of this sonnet.
The quatrains are all self-contained: the first two lines of each
establishes a premise, then is separated from the remaining
two lines with a semicolon; the third line begins with 'So'
followed by a verb to respond to that premise; and each
quatrain is closed with a concluding thought and a full stop.
All three quatrains have a nostalgic, defeatist tone.
The capping couplet is a volta that provides antithesis
to the preceding nostalgia.

There is a belief that the capping couplet of a good sonnet
should be able to stand alone. Its meaning should be robust
enough to work in isolation. I'm not sure I always achieve
that, but, in this case, I feel I do.

Our Chance

I worried that my world would detonate
Like a grenade, pin pulled, dropped in my lap;
So crushed my hands in prayer to abdicate
The guilt I felt for causing that mishap.
I felt an anchor round my ankles tied
With twisted twine that time would turn to wire;
So grabbed a coward's cutlass, then dry-eyed
Hacked at our bond of friendship and desire.
I failed to see the invite in your eyes
Because I thought it was not there for me;
So sought instead a sign to advertise
In neon, without doubt, a vacancy.
   I don't look back to gape, I merely glance
   We had time on the floor, we had our dance.

This sonnet is written to an "Old friend" who "chose a [different] path" to the speaker.

Each quatrain is sculpted around a different metaphor: the first is a damaged heart developing a crusty "shell"; the second a turncoat switching loyalty; the third two journeys heading in different directions.

All three quatrains are accusatory – with the speaker blaming the addressee for pain that "twisted" their "spirit". In the capping couplet, however, the speaker admits their "fate was earned".

Burnt

Old friend, your shoulder frost bit at my heart
Turned red flesh black at its extremities:
A crust that hardened as we moved apart;
A shell of gnarly bark from aged oak trees.
Before you turned your jacket inside out
I thought we marched with uniformity
But when your lining treachery did tout
My spirit twisted to deformity.
You chose a path that would not meet with mine
You took a bearing I could not pursue
I knew not then how that call would define
My willingness to seek close friends anew.
       Although your ice has left my fingers burned
       I got what I deserved; my fate was earned.

This sonnet is packed with rhetorical questions and juxtapositions; these techniques are the perfect tools for sharing the conflict and confusion of the narrative.

Each line in the first quatrain contains a juxtaposed pair: "bonds ... chains", "break ... escape", "loss ... gains", "vellum ... crepe". However, on close inspection, there is also ambiguity. Although "bonds" can be strong, positive connections, they can also be tethers. A "break" can be a prison break, or something that breaks. It can also be a holiday, respite.

The second quatrain is comprised of four (or five, depending on how dependent you judge the clauses in line seven to be) rhetorical questions. These are appeals to the addressee that will never be answered: such is the nature of poetry.

The final quatrain presents metaphors of freedom that become increasingly ominous. The first line is literal and so contains no linguistic suggestion of malignance. However, line eleven uses the phrase "out at sea" which could mean escape, but idiomatically means lost.

The capping couplet was the hardest to write. Caesura in the final line "dream. And" gives the summary the finality I wanted to sculpt.

My Butterfly

What I saw as proud bonds, you saw as chains
   What to me was a break was your escape
What I struck as a loss you weighed as gains
Our vellum history books, you felt, were crepe.
How long did you pretend that all was well?
Did carrying that burden twist your spine?
Was time with me a torment, was it hell?
Was I a fool to ever think you mine?
Well now you're independent, now you're free
Your wings have been unclipped, you've shed your reins
You've fled from Alcatraz, you're out at sea
On your clean slate no dust of me remains.
   For years I yearned for my bright butterfly
   Now I've released that dream. And watched it die.

Writing is an indulgent pastime: I spend precious time sculpting my thoughts, I unashamedly share them with others, then I hope for approval. Because I write to express personal truths, my writing isn't always easy to read. So, thank you to those who support me.

This sonnet is both self-indulgent and self-critical: it looks back at a time when I thought myself "a sage" when I was in fact "undeveloped". It is a letter to someone who offered "sunshine" that could not "penetrate the shell" I was unaware, at the time, I wore.

This confused (or changing) self-knowledge is represented by a mixture of congruous and incongruous positioning of the personal pronoun "I". At times it seems I know where to place the "I", others I don't.

Me not You

When whispered I, "It's me, it isn't you,"
　　Thought I the words I hissed were justified –
A valve undone enough to let lies through;
But retrospect reveals, I had not lied.
Your sunshine could not penetrate the shell
I did not know I'd lived my life within;
Your lava love to me was fiery hell
Too fierce for my underdeveloped skin.
How were you so mature when still so young?
How so together, how so sure of heart?
When I a fool spouting with serpent's tongue
Thought myself wise; a sage, seasoned and smart.
　　　　Lone hindsight words are lame apology
　　　　But you enrich my love anthology.

Similes are great, but this sonnet is all metaphors. Ten of them. The addressee is continually transformed into loud and "garish" things, some objects, some people. They "stand out", sometimes as an inappropriately dressed guest, sometimes as a 'Sore Thumb'. Saying the addressee is 'like' other things or acts 'as' them is inadequate. This person doesn't behave like inappropriate things, this person is inappropriate. Gleefully so.

The three quatrains have different out-of-place foci: noises; appearances and behaviours; characteristics. They're not silos: these out-of-place qualities are interwoven.

The capping couplet continues the personal criticism, leaving it as late as possible to deliver the rebuttal.

Sore Thumb

Y ou are the cymbals of a symphony
  Crashed out of time when all should be dulcet,
The choral singer harming harmony,
A foghorn at a proper lord's banquet.
You're a hot air balloon breaking blue sky
Gasping and garish, scaring tweeting flocks,
You don a clown suit when dress is black tie,
At a chilled soiree you're Jack-in-the-box.
When others mousely wait you bang the drum,
You're a black ram on white-sheep common ground,
You stand out like a proudly hammered thumb,
You're a bright nugget in a gravel mound.
        You struggle to conform; you have no clue:
        It's why I love, respect and value you.

This final 'love letter' fuses the power of love with the power of religion: Christian and Ancient Greek. It alludes to the work of the master of sonnets (William Shakespeare): "mortal coil", "milk of human kindness". More significantly, it compares the experience of being "caged" to that of being in love.

Overall, the poem functions similarly to an extended litotes: a negative statement used to assert a positive meaning. One of my favourite poems is 'To My Valentine' by Ogden Nash: "More than a catbird hates a cat … That's how much I love you." Which also (sort of) functions as an extended litotes.

The capping couplet of this sonnet concludes with a sentiment that could be interpreted as countering the suggestion (by Maya Angelou and others) that a "caged" bird suffers torment. However, this repost is unintended. The suggestion here is that the speaker prefers being "caged than far apart" from the addressee. The metaphor uses aversion to being "snared" to prove the intensity of the love. (In a litotes-type way.)

Caged

Why gave I you the pow'r to spin my world?
Let you jerk puppet me with nailed-on twine?
I am a worm around your finger curled,
In mortal coil seeking comfort divine.
When you a siren sang, I changed my course
When you shoved in a hook, I took the bait
When tipsters tipped the wink, I backed you horse;
A frozen Arctic fox, I sought you mate.
But soulless vacuum's the alternative
Or faux heart crudely stitched with fool's gold thread:
Both traps for innocents' desires to live
Whilst milk of human kindness being fed.
You lured, snared, grabbed, secured my yearning heart,
But I'm more happy caged than far apart.

About the author

I have been writing poetry since nursery [rhymes]. I also write short stories and novels.

My first collection of short fiction, 'My Goat Ate Its Own Legs', was published the UK, US and France.

I write to reflect on what it means, for me, to be human: truth and isolation are key themes. It is my hope that others will find my reflections entertaining and engaging… thought provoking, even.

- My Goat Ate Its Own Legs: debut collection of short fiction.
- A damaged boy: second collection of short fiction.
- The Titans: novel that examines the relationship between truth and megalomania.
- Axel is Free: supernatural sequel to The Titans, set amongst sentient mountains (Brecon Beacons).
- Outstared by a Bullfrog: novel that challenges the fallacy of an omnipotent god.
- Mr Livchild: novel set in the coming corpocracy.
- Fedw: debut poetry collection.
- The Year My Tears Failed: five short stories and five poems about human struggles.
- Up the Old Road: poems performed in a pub.
- Gothic Reflections: Gothic novella.
- Rewarding Behaviour: a non-fiction proposal for a more rewarding monetary system.

Connect with me online using:
My website: alexburrett.com
Twitter: @AuthorABurrett
Sonnet project: www.lovessonnets.com

Printed in Great Britain
by Amazon